BILL BRADLEY

SCHOLAR, ATHLETE, STATESMAN

TRICIA ANDRYSZEWSKI

A GATEWAY BIOGRAPHY

The Millbrook Press   Brookfield, Connecticut

AUTHOR'S NOTE ON SOURCES

Most of the quotations I've used in this book come from Bill Bradley's two memoirs, *Life on the Run* (New York: Vintage Books, 1995) and *Time Present, Time Past* (New York: Vintage Books, 1997), and from John McPhee's book about Bradley at Princeton, *A Sense of Where You Are* (New York: Noonday Press, 1978). Other books I've used in my research include Bradley's *Values of the Game* (New York: Artisan Press, 1998), William Jaspersohn's *Senator: A Profile of Bill Bradley in the U.S. Senate* (New York: Harcourt Brace Jovanovich, 1992), and Jon C. Halter's *Bill Bradley: One to Remember* (New York: G.P. Putnam's Sons, 1975). I've also consulted various newspaper and magazine articles, faxes sent to me by the Bradley presidential campaign's headquarters, and the campaign's Web site (www.billbradley.com). In addition, I followed Bill Bradley on the campaign trail in New Hampshire for a day in January 1999.

Library of Congress Cataloging-in-Publication Data
Andryszewski, Tricia, 1956-
Bill Bradley : scholar, athlete, statesman / by Tricia Andryszewski.
p.   cm.
Includes bibliographical references and index.
Summary: Follows the life of William Bradley, from his childhood in Missouri through his basketball career to his life in politics.
ISBN 0-7613-1669-8 (lib. bdg.) – ISBN 0-7613-1328-1 (pbk.)
1. Bradley, Bill, 1943- Juvenile literature. 2. Legislators–United States Biography. Juvenile literature. 3. United States. Congress. Senate Biography. Juvenile literature. [1. Bradley, Bill, 1943- . 2. Legislators. 3. Basketball players.] I. Title. II. Series.
E840.8B67A83 1999
328.73'092
[B]–DC21 99-28668 CIP

Cover photograph courtesy of AP/Wide World Photos
Photographs courtesy of AP/Wide World Photos: pp. 1, 18, 38, 39, 41, 43;
Seth Poppel Yearbook Archives: p. 10; Corbis/Bettmann-UPI: pp. 13, 21, 23, 28, 33, 35; © Benno Friedman/Outline Press: p. 31

Published by The Millbrook Press, Inc.
2 Old New Milford Road
Brookfield, CT 06804
Visit us at our Web site: http://www.millbrookpress.com.

CONTENTS

1
GROWING UP

"With the help of his friends, Bill could very well be president of the United States. And without the help of his friends he might make it anyway."

BILL BRADLEY'S HIGH SCHOOL PRINCIPAL

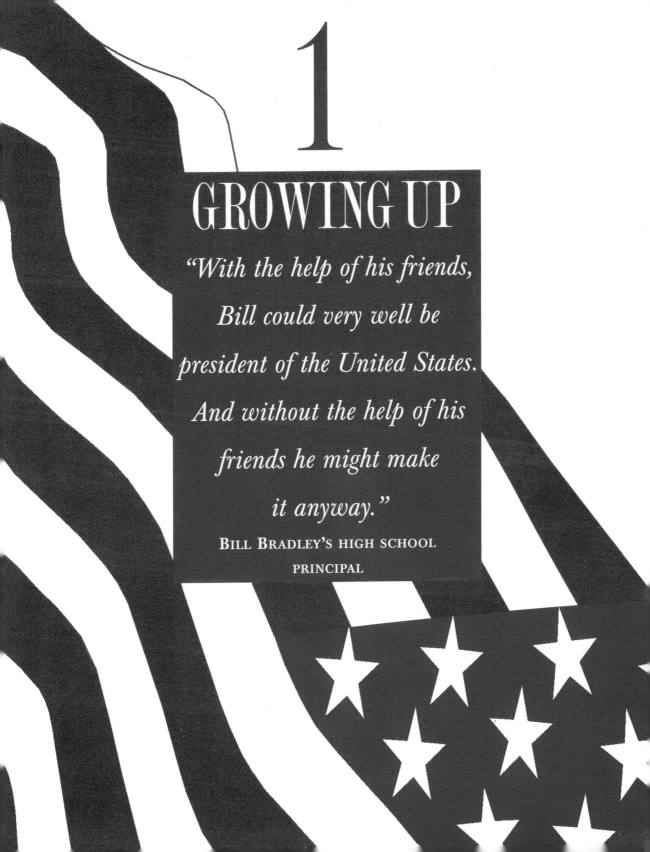

Bill Bradley was born on July 28, 1943, in Crystal City, Missouri. Crystal City was a small town on the banks of the Mississippi River, about 30 miles (48 kilometers) south of the big city of St. Louis. The town was so small it had only one traffic light. About 3,500 people lived there when Bill Bradley was growing up. Most of the men worked in the Pittsburgh Plate Glass factory by the river.

Bill Bradley's parents were older than most parents. His father, Warren, was forty-three when Bill was born. His mother, Susie, was thirty-five. Bill was their only child.

Warren Bradley grew up in Crystal City. When Warren was in tenth grade, his father died of cancer. Warren had to quit school to help support his family. First he worked for a railroad and then for the local bank in Crystal City. (His first job there was "shining pennies," he used to say.) Warren Bradley worked hard. Over the years he was promoted many times. Eventually, he was made president of the bank.

Warren Bradley had arthritis, high blood pressure, and other health problems. But that didn't stop him. His son Bill later wrote, "He walked to work every morning at 8:15 and back every evening at 5:15."

Bill's mother grew up in Herculaneum. This factory town was a few miles up the Mississippi River from Crystal City. Susie played basketball in high school. She went on to college and then became a schoolteacher. She gave up teaching and moved to Crystal City when she married Warren.

Bill Bradley lived with his parents in a nice house in the center of town. It was close to Bill's father's bank. The family went to Grace Presbyterian Church, right across the street from their house. Susie taught Sunday school, directed the youth choir, and taught summer Bible school.

Bill's mother had him take all kinds of lessons—French, swimming, basketball, boxing, piano, trumpet, and French horn. (He would have taken dancing lessons, too, but his father said no.) "My mother always wanted me to be a success," he says. "My father always wanted me to be a gentleman. Neither wanted me to be a politician."

Bill also found time to explore the limestone cliffs along the river near his home. He crawled into caves and found fossils of ferns and old Indian arrowheads. And he took walks with his stepgrandfather along the railroad tracks by the river.

Bill was keen to learn about the world outside his small town. "In our basement were stacks of old *Life* and *Look* magazines from as far back as 1938," he writes. "They smelled of mildew and age, but I sat looking through them for hours at a stretch. By the time I was thirteen, I had read and reread them all. The Second World War came to life in the war pictures in the magazines. . . . Pictures in *National Geographic* of Asian cities and African veldt, of the ruins of ancient civilizations, of natural wonders like the Amazon, Victoria Falls, Mt. Everest, the Nile, all lived in my imagination. Every time I put the magazines away and climbed back upstairs, I had the same thought: When will I ever visit those places in person?"

Bill played Little League baseball. But the game he really loved was basketball. He played it for the first time when he was nine, at the Crystal City YMCA. His mother soon put a basket on the side of their garage. Bill used to play with his friends or practice alone for hours and hours.

EVERY WINTER, Warren and Susie Bradley went to Palm Beach, Florida. When he was young, Bill always went along with them. But he missed his friends and basketball. The game wasn't played at the private school he went to when the family was in Florida. The winter Bill was in eighth grade, his parents let him stay home in Crystal City instead of going to Florida.

By then, Bill was 6 feet 3 (190 cm). The town's high- school coach already had his eye on him. (The coach wanted Bill to be a football star, but Bill wanted to play basketball.) The next year,

Bill went to high school. Ninth-grade students weren't usually put on the high-school basketball team. But that year the team lost its first four games. Then the coach decided to let Bill play. The team won sixteen of its next twenty-one games.

Bill practiced hard. Every day after school, he practiced basketball for more than three hours. He worked even more on Saturdays and Sundays. And he practiced three hours a day all summer. At a summer basketball camp he met Ed Macauley. Ed was a former pro player. He told Bill, "When you are not practicing, just remember—someone, somewhere, is practicing, and when you two meet, given roughly equal ability, he will win."

Bill also did cross-country training. "I ran from my home past the city's water-filtration plant," he wrote, "and onto a gravel road along the cracked mud fields [of farmland by the river], through the cottonwood trees to the edge of the Mississippi. There, before I ran back, I would stop for a few minutes and watch the river flow. No one swam in the river. The whirlpools made it too dangerous."

One summer Bill drove to a gym in St. Louis twice a week. There he played basketball games with college and pro players. Once, he says, "Zelmo Beatty, a six-foot-nine, two-hundred-forty-pound [206-cm, 109 kg) professional center, split my face open with an elbow . . . . The St. Louis Hawks' doctor had to stitch it up." By then, Bill himself was 6 feet 5 (196 cm)—his full adult height.

There was more to Bill Bradley's life in high school than just hoops. He studied. He got involved in student government. He became an Eagle scout. And, like his mother, he was religious.

Bill Bradley in a photograph taken for his high-school yearbook. The caption under the photo notes he was voted Most Popular and Best Athlete.

During Bill's junior year in high school, he went to a Fellowship of Christian Athletes conference in Wisconsin. Christian preachers ran this meeting. They believed that the most important thing you can do in life is to love Jesus and tell the world about it. Bill listened to the Christian-athlete speakers at the conference. It gave him new, strong feelings about religion. When he went home, he started to talk about Jesus to his teammates. He also talked to people at his family's church. He wanted to help people feel the way he did about God.

When Bill was a high-school senior, someone asked him who his heroes were. He listed Christian preacher Billy Graham, basketball star Bob Pettit, and Mark Hanna. Hanna was an Ohio politician who had a big influence on how presidential campaigns are run today.

Bill's parents were Republicans, and so was Bill through high school. But he wasn't very interested in politics. "My life was playing basketball, choosing a college, and doing well enough in school to have a choice," he said.

In his last year of high school, Bill had a great basketball season. His team made it into the playoff for the state championship. They were from a small school in a small town. (There were only ninety-six kids in Bill's high-school graduating class.) The other team was from a big school in St. Louis. "The big city makes you feel 'behind' if you come from a small town," Bill wrote. "The challenge was to show the world that we could compete against the big-city schools." Crystal City had beat the St. Louis team earlier that year. Bill and his teammates knew they could win the championship. But they lost—by just one point.

IN BETWEEN BALL GAMES, Bill thought hard about choosing a college. Because he was such a good ballplayer, dozens of colleges had offered him sports scholarships. (These were offers to pay for college if he would play for the school's basketball team.) Bill's mother wanted him to go to "Mizzou," the University of Missouri. Bill's father liked Princeton University in New Jersey. Princeton was an Ivy League school, along with Harvard, Yale, and a few others. Princeton offered an excellent education but no basketball scholarships. Bill chose Duke University, in Durham, North Carolina. And that college gave him a basketball scholarship.

During the summer after high-school graduation, Bill's father sent him to Europe. There he went on a tour with other college-age kids. One of the stops on the tour was Oxford University. Oxford is one of England's two best schools. Bill loved Oxford. And there he learned about Rhodes Scholars: After four years of college, excellent American students can apply to be Rhodes Scholars. Only a few are accepted, and they get to go to Oxford for two years. Bill thought he'd like to be a Rhodes Scholar someday.

When Bill returned from Europe, he broke his foot. He couldn't play basketball for a few weeks. He started to think about what his life might be like after he could no longer play. (Basketball is a young person's game. And a serious injury can end a player's career at any time.) Then Bill learned that Princeton sent more Rhodes Scholars to Oxford than any other college.

Bill thought about this until just days before he was supposed to leave for Duke. At the last minute he decided to go to Princeton instead. He moved to New Jersey and started classes in the fall of 1961.

COLLEGE

"Others can run faster and jump higher. The difference between Bill and other basketball players is self-discipline."

BILL BRADLEY'S COACH
AT PRINCETON

Bill Bradley had a tough time during his first year at Princeton. He almost flunked French. He said he was "always doubtful that a small-town boy could make it there. Many of my classmates were from prep schools [private schools that prepare kids for college] and had covered the first year's classwork the year before," he explained. "I was from a small-town high school in the Midwest and Ivy League standards were new to me and very, very difficult. Spring midterms went badly, so I quit freshman baseball—my second sport—and virtually lived in the library. I barely made it through that first year."

But he learned how to study. He often stayed up late at night after several hours of basketball practice. He kept this up for the rest of his time in college. And he did much better in his schoolwork after freshman year.

Meanwhile, Bradley was doing well on the basketball court. Freshmen don't play on Princeton's varsity basketball team, so he played with other freshmen. He was such a good player that At one point, he made fifty-seven foul shots in a row. That broke a basketball record set by a pro player.

In his sophomore year, Bradley joined the varsity team. He averaged twenty-seven points per game. People thought he was already the best basketball player ever to play for an Ivy League school. And he got better. In his junior and senior years he averaged more than thirty points per game. And if he hadn't passed the ball to other players so much, he would have scored even more!

BASKETBALL IS A TEAM GAME. Imagine that you've got the ball. But your teammate has a better shot at the basket. What do you do? You pass the ball to your teammate. Bill Bradley learned to play the game this way in high school. He kept playing that way even when he was a star on the court. He'd pass the ball to teammates closer to the basket even if he was more likely to sink the shot himself. (He was a much more accurate shooter than anyone he played with in high school or college.) This sometimes made coaches and fans crazy. Only late in a game, if his team was losing, would Bradley take more shots himself. He would do that to score enough points for the team to win.

Bill Bradley went to church while he was at Princeton. He taught Sunday school at a local church—even after getting home very late after a Saturday night away game. Meanwhile he became well known as a basketball star. Because of this Bill was asked to speak at more and more church gatherings. He gave speeches at churches around New Jersey and to Fellowship of Christian Athletes groups around the country.

But there were things about his church that were bothering Bill. He felt that many evangelical Christians were not tolerant of people who thought differently. And he was surprised and upset that many white Christians did not support the civil rights movement of the day. This movement was working to gain rights for African Americans. Bradley didn't understand "how those who professed such faith in Jesus Christ could . . . refuse to see that prejudice and discrimination against black people were affronts [insults] to Christian values."

The summer of 1964 was before Bill's senior year at Princeton. That summer he went to Washington to work for several Republican politicians. But during this summer, Bill Bradley became a Democrat. In June, he watched the U.S. Senate debate and pass the Civil Rights Act. This act made many kinds of unequal treatment against the law. "I remember thinking, America is a better place because of this bill," he later said. "All Americans—white or black—are better off." The Civil Rights Act was started by a Democratic president. More Democrats favored it than Republicans. Bill Bradley had been agreeing with the Democratic party more and more for several years. The Civil Rights Act made him decide to become a Democrat.

During that summer in Washington, Bradley also studied. He did research for his senior thesis. This was a big, book-length paper he'd have to write before graduating from Princeton.

Because he started work on his thesis ahead of time, Princeton let Bradley miss classes in the fall to go to Japan for the Olympics.

Bill Bradley was the youngest member of the U.S. Olympic basketball team that year. And he was captain of the team. The trip to Tokyo was his first time in Asia. "I hit my head constantly on doorframes and subway entrances [built for shorter people]," he wrote. "I got used to ducking. I didn't get used to the Japanese laughing and pointing at the giants walking down the street." Bradley and his teammates won the Olympic gold medal for basketball. After the Olympics, Bradley toured Taiwan and Hong Kong. He saw tourist sights and spoke to church groups.

Just before leaving for the Olympics, Bradley had mailed his application to be a Rhodes Scholar. Soon after he got back, he heard that he was accepted. He was going to be a student at Oxford University!

By this time, Bradley was receiving dozens of letters a day. Most of these letters were from strangers impressed with his basketball playing. Many asked him to speak at churches or to youth or business groups. Lots of people thought that Bill Bradley might someday become president of the United States—or at least governor of his home state, Missouri. The more famous Bradley became, the more people expected of him. He knew he could never do all that was asked of him. As time went on, he started to hate the attention.

Meanwhile, his basketball playing got better and better. He was named an All-American three years in a row. At the end of

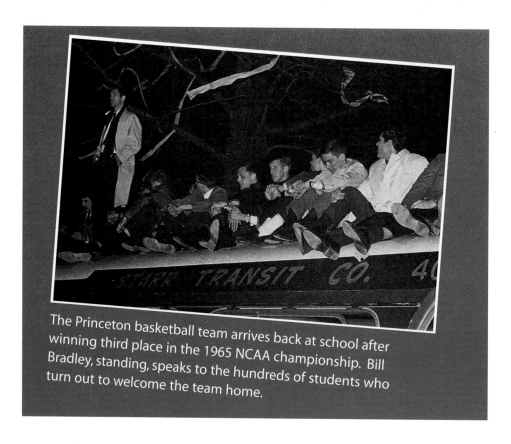

The Princeton basketball team arrives back at school after winning third place in the 1965 NCAA championship. Bill Bradley, standing, speaks to the hundreds of students who turn out to welcome the team home.

his senior season, he scored fifty-eight points in one game. This was a new record for most points scored by one player in an NCAA (National Collegiate Athletic Association) tournament game. The National Association of Basketball Coaches named him 1965 college player of the year.

THE NEW YORK KNICKERBOCKERS (Knicks) pro basketball team had kept a close watch on Bill Bradley through his college career. Princeton is only 60 miles (97 kilometers) or so from New York City. They wanted him to come play for them after college. They were stunned when he told them he was going to Oxford instead.

At Oxford, few people followed American basketball. Bradley liked that. His basketball fame had taken away his privacy, and he missed it. When he left for Europe, he told himself he was "finished with basketball." But he wasn't. The summer after his graduation from Princeton, in 1965, Bill Bradley traveled to Finland, Czechoslovakia, and Hungary for the World University Games. He and the U.S. basketball team won the gold medal. Even after settling in at Oxford, Bradley went to Italy twice a month to play with an Italian basketball team competing for the European Cup.

Mostly, though, Oxford was a great change for Bradley. It gave him a chance to do new things. He stopped practicing basketball. He read lots of books on subjects he'd never had time for before. He traveled all over Europe and the Middle East. He went to Italy, Spain, France, Switzerland, East and West Germany, Poland, Czechoslovakia, Hungary, the Soviet Union (including Russia, Belarus, and Ukraine), Yugoslavia, Syria, Israel, Lebanon, and Jordan. One year, he spent Christmas in Bethlehem and Jerusalem.

While he was at Oxford, Bradley became more and more uncomfortable with the mostly white, well-off Christian church groups he had grown up with. He spoke to an audience of several thousand people at a Billy Graham Christian "crusade" in

London. But the words no longer felt right in his mouth. "Then, one Sunday, in the church I attended at Oxford, the minister preached a sermon defending white racist rule over blacks in southern Africa," Bradley recalls. "I walked out, never to return."

Bradley's attitude toward professional basketball also changed while he was at Oxford. "Toward the end of my second year [at Oxford], after not touching a basketball for nine months, I went to the Oxford gym simply for some long overdue exercise. There I shot alone—just the ball, the basket, and my imagination. . . . I heard the swish and felt my body loosen into familiar movements—the jumper, the hook, the reverse pivot. . . . I realized that I missed the game." Bradley knew he still wanted to play. And he wanted to play against the best. "Three weeks later I signed a contract with the New York Knicks."

Bradley decided to put off his final exams at Oxford. Instead, he planned to complete six months of military service, play pro basketball in the 1967–1968 season, and then return to take his exams and get his degree.

The reason for this plan was the Vietnam war. The United States had set up a draft (required military service). Every young man who was physically fit and free to serve was on a list to be called up. (College students could only delay their service.) After he left Oxford, Bradley expected the U.S. military would call on him, too. By then, though, he felt that U.S. troops didn't belong in Vietnam. Bill Bradley didn't join the hundreds of thousands of Americans who publicly spoke out against the war. But he did

The original caption on this 1966 photograph notes that the 6-foot-5 Bradley had to duck through the archways at Oxford University.

decide to find a way to serve in the military without going to Vietnam.

Bradley joined the Air Force Reserve. He went on "active duty" as a personnel officer at McGuire Air Force Base in Wrightstown, New Jersey. He was there for six months in 1967. After that, he had reserve duty for one weekend a month for the next five years (plus two weeks each summer). In December 1967, at the end of his six months of active duty, Bill Bradley went to New York. He began his pro basketball career with the Knicks.

THE KNICKS

"For eight months you play basketball and think about basketball; your happiness depends on basketball. Then it is over."

BILL BRADLEY ON THE
PRO BASKETBALL SEASON

Bill Bradley joined the Knicks at mid-season, in December 1967. His first contract with them gave him $500,000 for four years of playing. (At that time, he says, the average pro basketball player's yearly pay was just $9,500.)

"Basketball was just a game . . . my father constantly reminded me," Bradley wrote. "When I first told him I was going to play professional basketball, he asked, 'When are you going to get a real job?' Then I told him what I would make playing pro ball. He replied . . . 'Not a bad job!'"

Bradley had to work hard for his pay. The Knicks played about a hundred games each season. And just after Bradley started, the team got a new coach. His name was Red Holzman. Holzman demanded dozens of practice sessions from the team.

Bradley wasn't a starting player his first season with the Knicks. He spent most of that year sitting on the bench. The coach sent more-experienced players out on the court to play the game. Bradley averaged just sixteen minutes of playing time a game.

Part of the problem was that Bradley was assigned to play guard. He just wasn't quick enough to be very good at it. He'd played forward in high school and college. But the Knicks already had a star forward, Cazzie Russell. Bradley's competition with Russell had begun back in 1964. That year, Bradley's Princeton team lost to Russell's University of Michigan team in a big game at Madison Square Garden. Now Russell had more pro experience than Bradley. Russell seemed to have a lock on the Knicks' forward position.

Bradley's first season as a pro ended in the spring of 1968. He went back to Oxford. There he studied hard for his exams for six weeks. In mid-June, he passed his exams. He now had a master's degree in politics, philosophy, and economics. After his exams, Bradley flew home to New York. For the rest of the summer he worked at the Urban League's Street Academy Reading Program in Harlem. He did office work and taught kids to read. Bradley also practiced basketball. He hoped to do better in his second year with the Knicks than he had in his first.

The basketball season started up again in the fall. By January 1969, "I had not yet broken into the Knicks' starting lineup," Bradley recalls. "I was failing as a guard; I was just too slow. Still, I refused to admit it, even to myself. In the January 21 game . . . Cazzie Russell broke his ankle. That gave me my chance to switch to forward, and, as they say in sports biographies, 'the rest was history.'" Bradley was short for a forward. But his generous and skillful teamwork brought out the best in himself and the other Knicks. He did well. For the next two years, Bradley and Russell took turns as starting forward.

As Bradley's playing improved, so did the Knicks. At the end of the 1969–1970 season, the Knicks won the NBA championship. Then, after the following season, the Knicks' coach traded Russell to San Francisco. Bradley had renewed his contract with the team. His rival was gone, and his place on the team was set as starting forward. Bradley relaxed and enjoyed the game a lot more. In 1973, he and the Knicks won the championship again.

PART OF BEING a professional basketball player is living eight months a year "in the rhythm of the road," as Bradley puts it—"a drive, a flight, a performance, a hotel, a sleep, and a drive, a flight, a return." You sometimes wake up in a hotel room and don't know which city you're in. You spend more time with your teammates—night and day—than you do with your family.

Bradley's teammates included some of the best-known players of that time: Willis Reed, Dick Barnett, Walt Frazier, Dave DeBusschere, and Earl Monroe. Most of his teammates were black. "Traveling with my teammates on the road in America was one of the most enlightening experiences of my life," he says. "I saw that if you're black in America, you never know when the next moment might bring a slight, a slur, or a slug."

His teammates nicknamed Bradley "Dollar Bill." This was partly because his first Knicks contract was for so much money.

It was also because he never seemed to spend much of it. He didn't buy fancy clothes or fancy cars. ("Bradley never has to worry about being mugged," one of his teammates said, "because he dresses as if he's already *been* mugged.") Bradley's teammates teased him. But they also sent "Dollar Bill" to represent them in the pro players union.

Bradley had decided before he signed his first contract with the Knicks that he wasn't going to do any commercial endorsements. (This means lending your name to advertising campaigns for shoes or clothes or other products.) He made this decision "to keep my experience of basketball pure," he said. "I felt about the court, the ball, and playing the way people feel about friends." Another reason was that he felt advertisers were interested in him more because he was a white player than because he was a good player. Bradley has said he could probably have earned about $50,000 a year from endorsements. Some players today earn millions.

When he first signed with the Knicks, Bradley thought that he'd play for just four years. That was the length of his first contract. Bradley knew that pro basketball was a young man's game. He wouldn't be able to play it forever. He started thinking seriously about politics as a post-basketball career. This began soon after the Knicks won the championship in 1970. He thought about returning to Missouri and running for some political office there. But, he found, "I had been away too long. I had lived in the East for over a decade, and now I felt more comfortable there

Bradley and Georgia State's Julian Bond played in an All-Star tournament. It was to benefit inner-city recreational and educational programs. Throughout his career, Bradley found time for charity work.

than in Missouri." He kept playing with the Knicks. Altogether, he played with them for ten seasons.

DURING HIS YEARS WITH THE KNICKS, Bradley sometimes traveled overseas during the off-season. He wanted to know more about the world and its people beyond the United States. He had wanted to do this since he was a kid back in Crystal City. "During the basketball season," he wrote, "I would [make] lists of interesting people in Kuala Lumpur or Bombay or Kabul. These were journalists, government officials, academics, businessmen, social activists. When I arrived in town, I'd call their offices . . . and ask if I could meet them."

While he was with the Knicks, Bradley met and married Ernestine Misslbeck Schlant. She was a single mother and a neighbor in his apartment building. Ernestine had grown up in West Germany, left college there, and come to America. She married young and had a child named Stephanie before getting divorced. She then went back to school and became a college professor. Bill Bradley and Ernestine were married in 1974. They bought a house and moved to New Jersey, where she continued to teach German literature. Their daughter, Theresa Anne, was born in 1976.

The same year Bradley got married, he thought again about retiring from the Knicks. He wanted to run for a seat in the U.S. House of Representatives from New Jersey. But that year he was also writing a book, *Life on the Run.* It was about life as a pro basketball player. He felt good about writing the book. And he was "still making good money playing a game I loved," he said. He decided to play basketball a while longer.

By 1976, Bradley had finished his book. "I was ready to move on to something else," he said. He was older and slowing down a bit on the basketball court. He decided to quit the Knicks after the 1976–1977 season and run for the U.S. Senate in 1978.

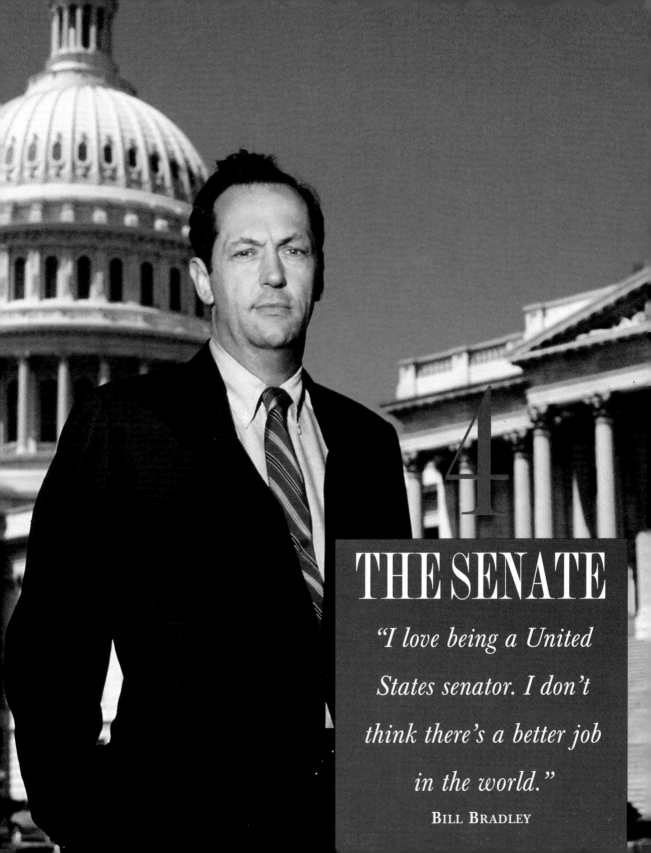

4

THE SENATE

"I love being a United States senator. I don't think there's a better job in the world."

BILL BRADLEY

U.S. senators hold one of the highest elected offices in the United States. Only the president and vice president are chosen by more voters. Most people who make it to the Senate work their way up in politics. They start out in local politics, then maybe their state's legislature, then possibly a state governorship or a seat in the U.S. House of Representatives.

Not Bill Bradley. He aimed straight for the Senate. In 1978 he asked the voters of New Jersey to elect him as one of their two senators. Bradley had no experience in government. But he did have some real advantages as a political candidate. He was famous, popular, and willing to spend some of his own money (from playing basketball) on his campaign. Voters seemed to like the fact that Bradley was a political "outsider." He won the election with 56 percent of the vote.

Bradley was thirty-five years old when he was sworn into office in the U.S. Senate. He was the youngest person then serving as a senator. He knew he had a lot to learn, and he worked hard to learn it. He attended all the meetings of the Senate committees he was assigned to. He read a lot about the things his

Vice President Walter Mondale swears in Senator Bradley, who holds two-year-old Theresa Anne. On Bradley's left are his wife, Ernestine, and his stepdaughter, Stephanie Schlant.

committees dealt with, especially energy policy, taxes, and trade. He also learned how laws are made in the Senate—getting senators to agree, asking them to vote with you on things you think are important. You need to know who will, who might, and who definitely won't go along with you. The Senate is run by a very complicated set of rules. Bradley learned that knowing how to play by the rules can mean the difference between success and failure.

Bradley also learned how important goodwill and respect are in the Senate. "There are only a hundred people in the [Senate]; most of them have a rather strong sense of themselves," he says. "None of them wants to be embarrassed, and all of them want to win—every time." Friendship and good manners help to keep disagreements from turning into long-term grudges.

IN THE SENATE, Bradley tried to solve big problems. "I always preferred trying for big reform," he says. "If you succeed with a small reform, all you get is a slightly different set of complaints and another, related task next year. If you succeed with big reform, you can change the country."

Perhaps the biggest and most complicated problem Bradley took on was tax reform. "After I was in the Senate for less than a year," he says, "I realized that most Americans paid at higher tax rates than necessary so that a much smaller group of Americans could take advantage of loopholes." (Loopholes are special breaks written into the tax rules for certain kinds of taxpayers.)

For years, Bradley talked about making the U.S. tax system fairer, simpler, and more efficient. He even wrote a book about it, called *The Fair Tax*. "When I worked for tax reform . . . I was thinking of the middle class," Bradley said. "Because of loopholes in the tax code, too many people with the same income paid different amounts of tax. I believed that many hardworking Americans would be better off if loopholes were fewer and rates were lower; that way, they could keep more of each additional dollar they earned, and equal incomes would pay about equal taxes."

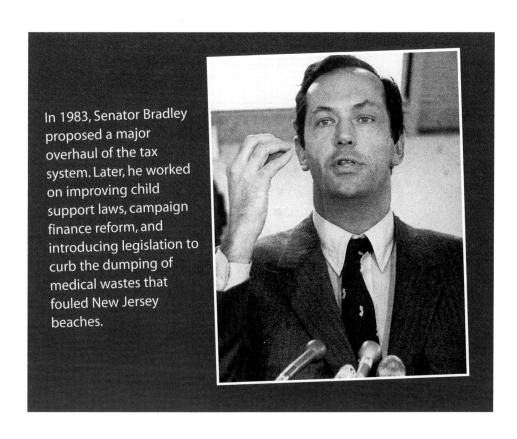

In 1983, Senator Bradley proposed a major overhaul of the tax system. Later, he worked on improving child support laws, campaign finance reform, and introducing legislation to curb the dumping of medical wastes that fouled New Jersey beaches.

In 1984, President Ronald Reagan proposed changing the tax system by closing loopholes and lowering tax rates. Reagan was a Republican, and Bradley was a Democrat. But Bradley strongly supported Reagan's Tax Reform Bill of 1986. He also talked other Democrats into supporting it. The Tax Reform Bill passed and became law. The top tax rate for individual taxpayers was cut almost in half. Enough loopholes were closed to bring in billions of dollars each year. (Unfortunately, senators and representatives made changes in the years after the Tax Reform Bill was passed. They put back their favorite loopholes in the tax code one by one. By the late 1990s, the tax code was once again far from fair, simple, and efficient.)

Senator Bradley took on lots of other issues. He worked to help the world's poorest countries grow economically. He also tried to reduce the amount of money they owed to richer countries. And he worked on water policy in the American West. There, he tried to make the rules about who can use how much water fairer to everyone—farmers, fishermen, city residents, and even wildlife. In addition, he served for eight years on the Senate Intelligence Committee. This group of senators oversees America's spies and other top-secret researchers.

Bradley also got to know the state of New Jersey. (He once made three round-trips between Washington and New Jersey in one day!) He met several times a year with groups of kids. He held a once-a-year class for high-school students. In this class, students played senator-for-a-day. They talked about how to deal with big issues like the U.S. government's budget and how America should deal with other nations. Bradley also often met with New Jersey voters in "walking town meetings." He'd go to a train station or a factory parking lot or a diner and talk to people about whatever they wanted to talk about. Many of these "walking town meetings" took place at the Jersey Shore. Every summer, Bradley spent several days walking and talking along the string of beaches where New Jersey meets the Atlantic Ocean.

Bradley easily won reelection to the Senate in 1984. But in 1990, he ran into trouble.

In 1990 the governor of New Jersey was Jim Florio, a Democrat. In June, Governor Florio pushed through a huge state tax increase. Voters got angry at all Democrats—even Bradley, who had nothing to do with the tax increase. Bradley almost lost the election that fall.

Bradley took this near-defeat personally. He felt hurt. "I looked at each person . . . as if he or she had voted against me," he said. But "in the long run, the close election was the best thing that ever happened in my political career. It forced me to face up to what I needed to change. . . . It forced me to go deeper into my emotions and to speak from values and convictions in ways I had avoided before."

ONE OF THE THINGS Bradley decided to change was the way he raised money for campaigning. He had begun raising money for his 1990 election campaign way back in 1985. Altogether he raised $12.9 million—a huge amount of money for a Senate race. Because of this, his opponent spoke badly of him. She said that Bradley raised a lot of money at the same time that he talked about limiting the money spent in political campaigns. After the election, Bradley took a long break from fundraising. And he worked with other senators to try to limit the money flowing into political campaigns.

After the 1990 election, Bradley also began to speak out on big national issues. One thing that concerned him was race relations in America. And he got better at letting the people of New

Bradley and his family—Stephanie, Ernestine, and Theresa Anne—celebrate his narrow victory over Christine Todd Whitman in 1990.

Jersey know about his work in the Senate. By the time he finished his annual summer beach walk in 1991, he was feeling better about himself. He also felt "close to the people of New Jersey."

Many of Bradley's friends and supporters had hoped that his 1990 reelection campaign would be a warmup. They wanted to see him run for president of the United States in 1992. But he barely won reelection to his Senate seat. Those presidential hopes faded.

Bradley had several personal reasons to be glad he wasn't running for president in 1992. In spring of 1992 his wife, Ernestine, learned that she had breast cancer and needed surgery. She also had six months of chemotherapy (a tough course of cancer-killing medicine). Breast cancer often kills, and the Bradleys didn't know whether she would survive.

Bradley with Ernestine in her office.

Meanwhile, the health of Bill's parents was worsening. Over the next two years, several people close to him died. In 1994, his father died. These events changed Bradley. Before, he said, "the thought that maybe there wouldn't be a tomorrow had never seriously occurred to me. Now it went with me everywhere."

"Everywhere" reached far beyond New Jersey and Washington. Part of a U.S. senator's job is campaigning for other politicians all over the United States. Since Bradley was once a popular basketball star, a lot of politicians wanted him to join them on the campaign trail. In 1992 alone, Bradley traveled to twenty-seven states. He campaigned that year for Democratic presidential candidate Bill Clinton and vice-presidential candidate Al Gore.

Soon after the 1992 election, Bill Bradley started writing another book. It is called *Time Present, Time Past*, and it is about being a senator. Writing down his thoughts led him to decide that it was time once again to move on. "So on August 16, 1995, I announced that I would not run for reelection to a fourth Senate term [in 1996]," he wrote. "I knew I had spent the last eighteen years where I wanted to be. I loved my job. . . . Yet . . . I longed for new horizons."

"Being a U.S. senator is the best elective job in the world," Bradley says. "It affords complete independence. A senator is accountable only to his conscience and the voters of his state, and then only once every six years. A senator sets his own schedule and determines his own style. A senator can call virtually any

Bradley on the publicity trail, instead of a campaign trail, signing copies of *Time Present, Time Past* at a bookstore.

American for advice and get it. . . . In the Senate, you know that you're in the middle of the action and that what you do has an impact."

Still, "the Senate is not the only place to serve," Bradley wrote in 1996, "I am leaving the Senate, but I am not leaving public life."

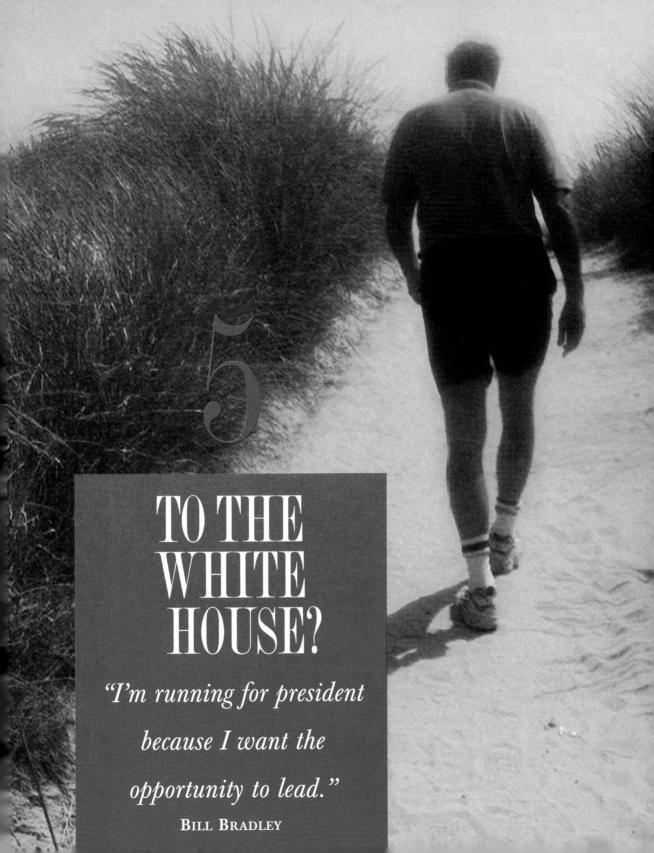

5

TO THE WHITE HOUSE?

"I'm running for president

because I want the

opportunity to lead."

BILL BRADLEY

Bill Bradley has said that if you run for president of the United States, you must at least:

(1) Know America well, firsthand, from traveling and talking with thousands of people. (2) Know a lot about the world outside the United States, so you can do a good job dealing with foreign countries. (3) Have a team of able and willing workers lined up to help you do your job after you're elected. (4) Be able to explain your ideas to the American people.

In 1988 and again in 1992, Bradley decided he wasn't ready to run for president. He wasn't sure he had mastered those four "musts." And he wasn't ready and willing to put himself and his family in the spotlight of a presidential campaign.

Democrat Bill Clinton was elected president in 1992. President Clinton ran for reelection in 1996. Other Democrats—including Bill Bradley—didn't challenge him, and Clinton won. But since the U.S. Constitution limits presidents to just two elected terms, President Clinton could not run again. American voters would choose a new president in 2000.

In December 1998, Bill Bradley said he would run. He was better prepared for being president and confident he could do the job well. His family was better prepared, too. His wife was healthy. She was no longer fighting the cancer that threatened her life in 1992. And his daughter, Theresa, was older.

In February 1999, Bradley made his first major speech of the 2000 presidential campaign. He spoke to a group of Democrats in Virginia about what the Democratic party should be trying to do. He talked about where he would lead the party (and America) if he were president. His key points included:

★ All Americans must have equal opportunity, no matter what the color of their skin.
★ Working families need better jobs and education and more help from the community.
★ Every American should have health insurance.
★ America should encourage democracy and peace all over the world.
★ Campaign finance rules should be changed, to shrink the role money plays in national politics.
★ Most of all, leaders should encourage Americans to take better care of each other and their communities.

"I want to be president because I know this is a great country and a great people," Bradley concluded. "I know that when we unleash our energy and creativity and intelligence, the great challenges facing us can be met—and triumphed over. I know that we can do all of this and more—as Democrats and as Americans."

Bradley faced a long, hard campaign. First, he would have to convince Democrats to select him instead of Al Gore as their candidate for president. Then, in November 2000, he would have to convince a majority of American voters to choose him as their next president.

During the campaign, Bill Bradley would tell the American public a lot more about what he would do if he were president. But what would Bill Bradley do if he lost the election?

"If I wasn't in politics," Bradley once told a group of high-school kids, "I'd probably write. I'd probably continue to work with young people. I'd probably—oh, I don't know, a number of things. You don't want to peek at all your cards. I've got a few."

TIMELINE

July 28, 1943 – Bill Bradley is born, in Crystal City, Missouri.

Spring 1961 – High-school graduation.

Fall 1961 – Starts college at Princeton University.

Summer 1964 – Works for politicians in Washington, D.C.

Fall 1964 – Wins a gold medal with the American basketball team at Tokyo Olympics.

Spring 1965 – Graduates from Princeton with honors in American history.

Fall 1965 – Arrives at Oxford University, in England, as a Rhodes Scholar.

Summer 1967 – Begins six-month tour of active duty in U.S. Air Force.

December 1967 – Starts playing for New York Knicks.

Summer 1968 – Earns graduate degree at Oxford.

1970, 1973 – Knicks win NBA championship.

1974 – Marries Ernestine Schlant.

1976 – Daughter, Theresa Anne, is born.

1977 – Retires from Knicks.

1978 – Elected U.S. senator from New Jersey.

1982 – Elected to Basketball Hall of Fame.

1996 – Retires from Senate.

December 1998 – Announces run for the U.S. presidency.

INDEX